P9-DVT-420

IGUANODON

by Sally Lee

CAPSTONE PRESS
a capstone imprint

Little Explorer is published by Capstone Press,
1710 Roe Crest Drive, North Mankato, Minnesota 56003
www.capstoneyoungreaders.com

Library of Congress
Cataloging-in-Publication Data

Lee, Sally, 1943– author.
Iguanodon / by Sally Lee.
pages cm. — (Smithsonian Little explorer.
Little paleontologist)
Summary: "Introduces young readers to Iguanodon,
including physical characteristics, habitat, diet, behavior,
and fossil discovery"— Provided by publisher.
Audience: Ages 4–7
Audience: K to grade 3.
Includes index.
ISBN 978-1-4914-2129-1 (library binding)
ISBN 978-1-4914-2376-9 (paperback)
ISBN 978-1-4914-2380-6 (paper over board)
ISBN 978-1-4914-2384-4 (eBook PDF)
1. Iguanodon—Juvenile literature. 2. Paleontology—
Cretaceous—Juvenile literature. 3. Dinosaurs—Juvenile
literature. I. Title.
QE862.O65L443 2015
567.914—dc23   2014021785

Editorial Credits

Michelle Hasselius, editor; Heidi Thompson, designer;
Wanda Winch, media researcher; Tori Abraham,
production specialist

Our very special thanks to Mike Brett-Surman, PhD,
Museum Specialist for Fossil Dinosaurs, Reptiles,
Amphibians, and Fish at the National Museum of
Natural History, Smithsonian Institution, for his
curatorial review. Capstone would also like to thank
Kealy Wilson, Product Development Manager, and the
following at Smithsonian Enterprises: Ellen Nanney,
Licensing Manager; Brigid Ferraro, Vice President,
Education and Consumer Products; Carol LeBlanc, Senior
Vice President, Education and Consumer Products.

Image Credits

Academy of Natural Sciences of Drexel University College
of Medicine, 28; Alamy: The Natural History Museum,
30–31; Bridgeman Images: Natural History Museum,
London, UK/John Sibbick, 24; Capstone Studio: Karon
Dubke, 13, Capstone, James Field, 5, 8–9; Corbis: James
L. Amos, 19 (bottom), Louis Psihoyos, 27, Stock Trek
Images/Phillip Brownlow, 22; Dreamstime: Corey A. Ford,
17 (middle); Jon Hughes, cover, 1, 4 (silhouette), 6–7, 10,
12–13, 14, 15, 16, 18–19, 20; Mary Evans Picture Library:
Natural History Museum, 25 (all); Science Source, 26
(all); Shutterstock: BACO, 4 (bus), Dan Collier, 9 (bottom
right), Dario Marelli, 7 (bottom right), leonello calvetti,
2–3, reallyround, 5 (bottom right), Steffen Foerster, 5
(bottom left), svetok30, 21, T4W4, 4 (folder), Volodymyr
Burdiak, 11 (br); Thinkstock: Dorling Kindersley, 17 (tl,tr),
John Temperton, 17 (b); Thomas Smith, 23; Wikipedia: Jes,
Melbourne, Australia, 29 (t), Illustrated Encyclopaedia of
Dinosaurs, 29 (b)

Printed in the United States of America in Stevens Point, Wisconsin.
032014   008092WZF14

TABLE OF CONTENTS

name: Iguanodon

how to say it: ih-GWAN-oh-don

when it lived: early Cretaceous Period, Mesozoic Era

what it ate: plants

size: 30 feet (9.1 meters) long
16 feet (4.9 m) tall
weighed 4 to 5 tons
(3.6 to 4.5 metric tons)

Iguanodon was a large plant-eating dinosaur that lived 125 million years ago. Iguanodon means "iguana tooth." The dinosaur's teeth looked like an iguana's, but they were much bigger.

Thanks to
FOSSILS

A fossil is evidence of life from the past. Fossils of things like bones, teeth, and tracks found in the earth have taught us everything we know about dinosaurs.

PREHISTORIC GIANT

long head

sharp beak

short front legs

thumb spike
on each hand

fused middle fingers

Iguanodon belonged to a group of dinosaurs called ornithopods. They ate plants and could walk on two legs.

stiff tail

strong back legs

giraffe

Iguanodon was as tall as a giraffe. It was as heavy as an elephant.

BALANCING ACT

Iguanodon had a stiff tail. It stuck straight out when the dinosaur walked or ran. Iguanodon used its tail to keep its balance. Iguanodon's tail kept the dinosaur from tipping over.

Iguanodon's tail wasn't always stiff. The dinosaur was born with a droopy tail that fit inside its egg. The tail slowly grew harder as Iguanodon got older.

Diplodocus

Many dinosaurs used their tails
for balance, such as Diplodocus.

POWERFUL LEGS

Iguanodon had three large, clawed toes on each back foot.

Iguanodon had strong back legs.
The back legs were much larger
than the front legs.

Iguanodon could walk on
its two back legs or on all
four. Iguanodon was taller
when it walked on its
back legs. This helped
the dinosaur see farther
away and spot predators.

kangaroo

Kangaroos can also walk
on two or four legs.

HANDY HANDS

Iguanodon's middle three fingers
fused together to form a pad
on each hand. The pads helped
the dinosaur walk on four legs.

Iguanodon's pinky fingers could bend in to touch the palms of its hands. The pinky fingers helped the dinosaur hold onto food.

Iguanodon had long spikes instead of thumbs. The spikes stuck straight out. They were sharp enough to stab a predator.

Iguanodon's thumb spikes grew up to 6 inches (15 centimeters) long. That's about as long as a U.S. dollar bill.

U.S. dollar

LONG HEAD

Iguanodon had a beak for a mouth
like a bird or turtle. Rows of teeth
lined the sides of Iguanodon's mouth.
The dinosaur had no front teeth.

Iguanodon could chew its food. Chewing made food easier to digest. Iguanodon chewed its food by moving its mouth from side to side.

Iguanodon's head was long like a horse's head. The dinosaur had a bigger brain than many other plant-eating dinosaurs.

CRETACEOUS HOME

Iguanodon lived in what is now Europe. But fossils from other ornithopods have been found on every continent except Antarctica.

Flowers grew for the first time during the Cretaceous Period.

The early Cretaceous Period was warm with wet and dry seasons. Plants and trees such as conifers, ginkgoes, and cycads grew easily.

Other Cretaceous Animals

Baryonyx

Polacanthus

Hypsilophodon

Cetiosaurus

The Cretaceous Period lasted from 145 million to 66 million years ago.

DINOSAUR ERA

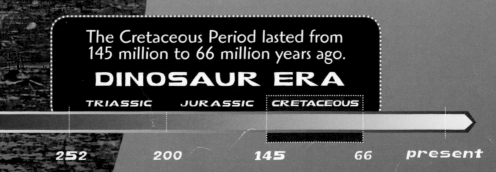

TRIASSIC	JURASSIC	CRETACEOUS	
252	200	145	66	present

millions of years ago

HERD LIFE

Iguanodon lived and traveled in herds to find food. Herds also kept the dinosaurs safe. Not many predators would attack a big group of giant dinosaurs.

Bone beds show that Iguanodon lived in herds. Iguanodon bone beds have been found in Belgium and Germany.

dinosaur bone bed at the Dinosaur National Monument in Utah

Bone beds are areas with a large number of fossils.

PLANT EATER

Iguanodon was
an herbivore. An
herbivore eats plants.

Iguanodon had more ways of getting food than most dinosaurs. It could bend down to eat low-growing cycads and ferns. It could also stand on its back legs to reach tall conifers and ginkgoes.

Like many plant eaters, Iguanodon spent most of its time eating. Iguanodon used its sharp beak to snip leaves off tough plants.

horsetails

Iguanodon also ate gritty horsetails.

DINOSAUR TRACKS

Trackways are sets of dinosaur footprints found in stone. They give scientists clues about how dinosaurs moved and lived.

Trackways show scientists that an adult Iguanodon mainly walked on four legs. But it ran on two legs.

Tracks that are spaced far apart show that a dinosaur was running. Some scientists think Iguanodon could run 9 to 12 miles (14.5 to 19 kilometers) per hour.

A relative of Iguanodon left trackways at Dinosaur Ridge in Colorado.

EGGS AND BABIES

Like all dinosaurs Iguanodon hatched from an egg. A female Iguanodon probably laid 12 to 24 eggs at a time.

a model of a dinosaur nest

Scientists aren't sure if females cared for their eggs and babies. So far no fossils of Iguanodon nests have been found.

Trackways show young Iguanodons traveled on two legs instead of four.

a model of dinosaur eggs and babies

Very few dinosaur babies became adults. Most were killed by predators.

ROCKS WITH TEETH

In 1822 Gideon and Mary Mantell found giant teeth in rocks near Sussex, England. They didn't know what animal the teeth came from. At that time no one knew about dinosaurs.

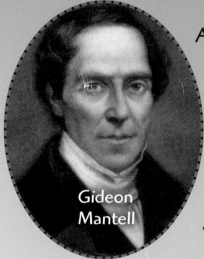

Mary Mantell

Gideon Mantell

At first scientists thought the teeth were from a rhinoceros or fish. But other people had also found large bones around this time. Scientists later discovered the bones were from dinosaurs.

"Discovery of these teeth ... really kickstarted the entire study of dinosaurs."
—Paul Barrett from the Natural History Museum

Gideon Mantell named Iguanodon in 1825. The word "dinosaur" was not created until 1842.

Iguanodon teeth discovered by Gideon and Mary Mantell

Iguanodon was the second dinosaur to be named. Megalosaurus was first.

DINNER IN THE DINOSAUR

Models of Iguanodon, Megalosaurus, and Hylaeosaurus were displayed in England in 1854. They were the first life-sized dinosaur models ever made. The models got people excited about dinosaurs.

Sculptor Benjamin Hawkins had scientists help him design the models. They made some mistakes. They put Iguanodon's thumb spike on its nose.

Benjamin Hawkins

Today scientists know the models are not right, but they are still popular. They are on display at Crystal Palace Park in England.

Iguanodon model (front) at Crystal Palace Park

Hawkins had a strange dinner party in 1853. The 21 guests ate inside the giant mold Hawkins used to make the Iguanodon model.

GLOSSARY

bone bed—a single layer of rock that contains a large number of fossils

conifer—a tree with cones and narrow leaves called needles

continent—one of Earth's seven large land masses

cycad—a plant shaped like a tall pineapple with palmlike leaves

digest—to break down food so it can be used by the body

fossil—evidence of life from the geologic past

ginkgo—a tree with green, fan-shaped leaves

herd—a group of animals that lives or moves together

horsetail—a plant with stems and tiny leaves; related to ferns

Mesozoic Era—the age of dinosaurs, which includes the Triassic, Jurassic, and Cretaceous periods; when the first birds, mammals, and flowers appeared

model—something that is made to look like a person, animal, or object

predator—an animal that hunts other animals for food

sculptor—a person who creates art by carving stone, wood, or other materials

trackway—a set of footprints from long ago found in rocks

CRITICAL THINKING USING THE COMMON CORE

Iguanodon could walk on two or four legs. Name an animal today that can walk on two or four legs. Use the text to help you with your answer. (Key Ideas and Details)

Scientists believe bone beds show Iguanodon lived in herds. What is a bone bed? (Craft and Structure)

Look at the Iguanodon model on page 29. Based on what we now know about Iguanodon, describe two things that should be changed on the model. (Integration of Knowledge and Ideas)

READ MORE

Dixon, Dougal. *Iguanodon and Other Leaf-Eating Dinosaurs*. Dinosaur Find. Minneapolis: Picture Window Books, 2009.

Raatma, Lucia. *Iguanodon*. Dinosaurs. Ann Arbor, Mich.: Cherry Lake Pub., 2013.

West, David. *Iguanodon: Iguana Tooth*. Graphic Dinosaurs. New York: PowerKids Press, 2012.

INTERNET SITES

FactHound offers a safe, fun way to find Internet sites related to this book. All of the sites on FactHound have been researched by our staff.

Here's all you do:

Visit *www.facthound.com*

Type in this code: 9781491421291

Super-cool stuff! Check out projects, games and lots more at
www.capstonekids.com

INDEX